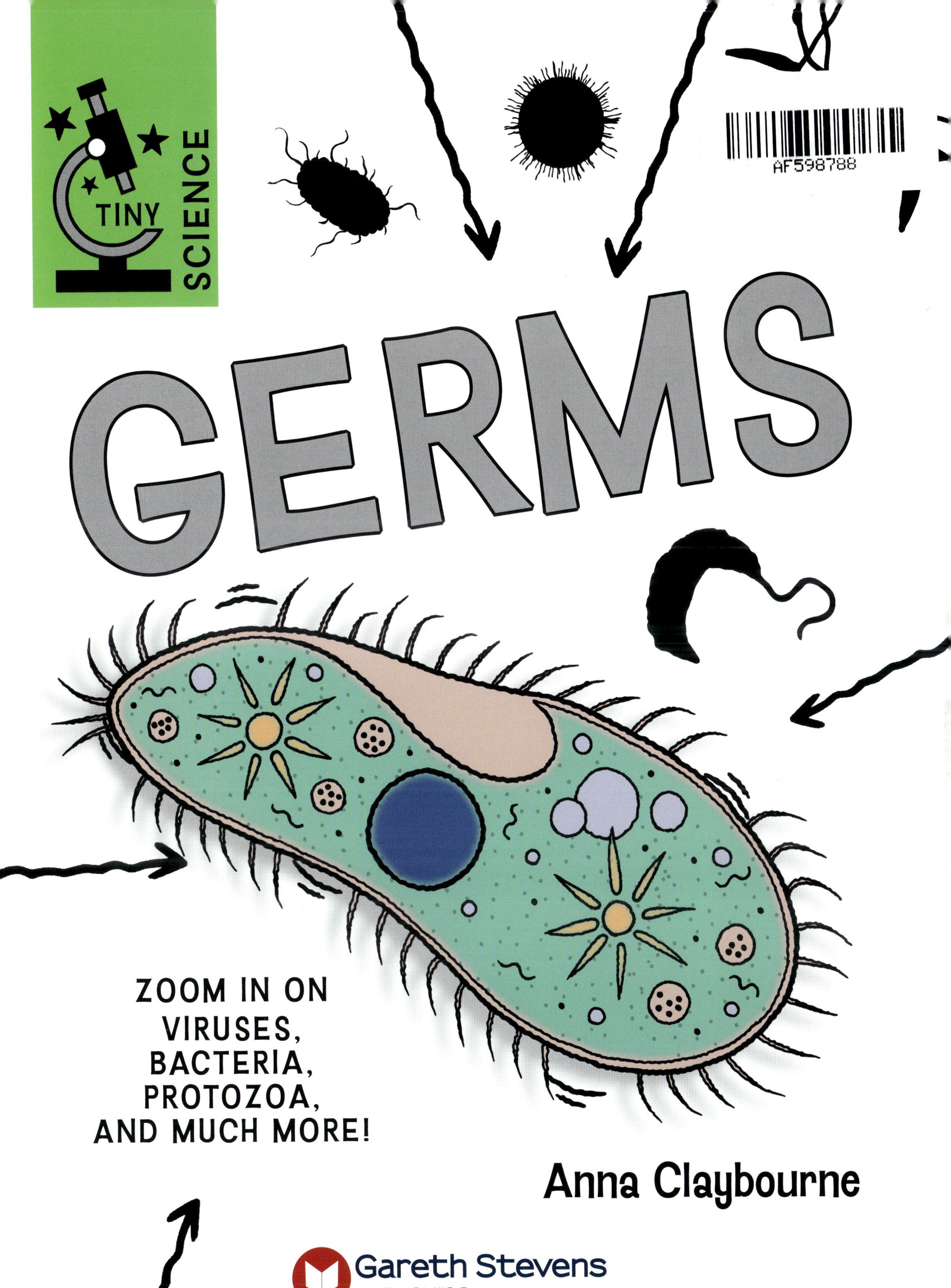
TINY
SCIENCE
GERMS
ZOOM IN ON VIRUSES, BACTERIA, PROTOZOA, AND MUCH MORE!
Anna Claybourne
Gareth Stevens
PUBLISHING

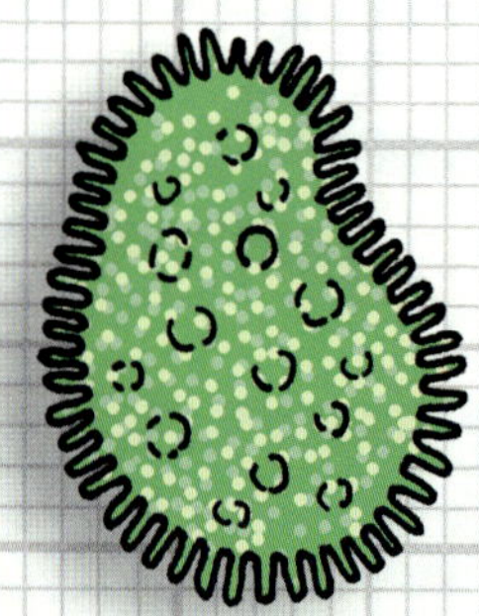

Please visit our website, www.garethstevens.com. For a free color catalog of all our high-quality books, call toll free 1-800-542-2595 or fax 1-877-542-2596.

Published in 2025 by
Gareth Stevens Publishing
2544 Clinton St.
Buffalo, NY 14224

First published in Great Britain in 2022 by Wayland

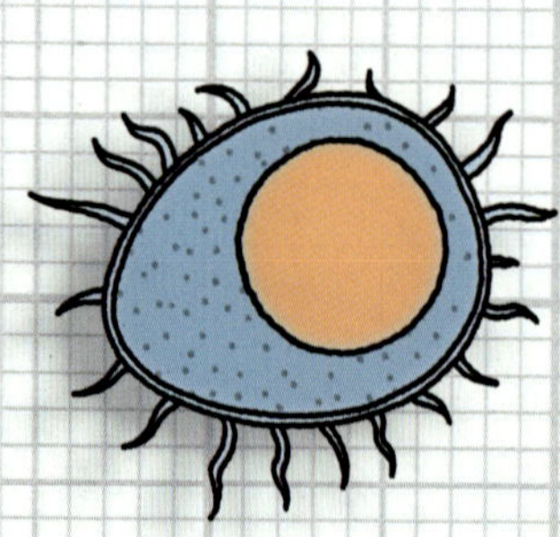

Editor:
Grace Glendinning

Design and illustrations:
Matt Lilly

Cover design:
Matt Lilly

Cataloging-in-Publication Data

Title: Germs / Anna Claybourne.
Description: Buffalo, NY : Gareth Stevens Publishing, 2025. | Series: Tiny science | Includes glossary and index.
Identifiers: ISBN 9781538294147 (pbk.) | ISBN 9781538294154 (library bound) | ISBN 9781538294161 (ebook)
Subjects: LCSH: Bacteria--Juvenile literature. | Microorganisms--Juvenile literature.
Classification: LCC QR74.8 C54 2025 | DDC 579.3--dc23

Alamy: Mediscan 6c, 14b; BSIP SA 12c; Science History Images 5.
Getty Images: James Cavallini/BSIP 4.
iStock: Christoph Burgstedt 21t; carroteater 9t; Dr Microbe 9c; Fotoedu 26b; Ilexx 8cl; Juan Ruiz Paramo 24c; Urfinguss 20c.
Science Photo Library: EM Unit, VLA 9b; Steve Gschmeissner 8br, 11b; Lee D Simon 12b.
Shutterstock: Africa Studio 11bc; Aslysun 25c; Cunaplus 18b; Diamant24 14tc; Everett Collection 25b; HollyHarry 24t; Innakreativ 14c; JBArt 7t; Kateryna Kon 11t,16, 25t; krakenimages.com 17b; Roland Magnusson 14tl; Nechaevkon 6br, 17tr; Igor Normann 26cl; Olhastock 26t; Schira 6bc; S-F 27b; Sruilk 18t; Taras Verkhovynets 14tr; Alex Visualnue 21c; Rudmer Zwever 7br.
Wikimedia Commons: Cynthia Goldsmith/CDCP/PD 25cr; Perugia/PD 7c.

Printed in the United States of America

CPSIA compliance information: Batch #CSGS25: For further information contact Gareth Stevens at 1-800-542-2595.

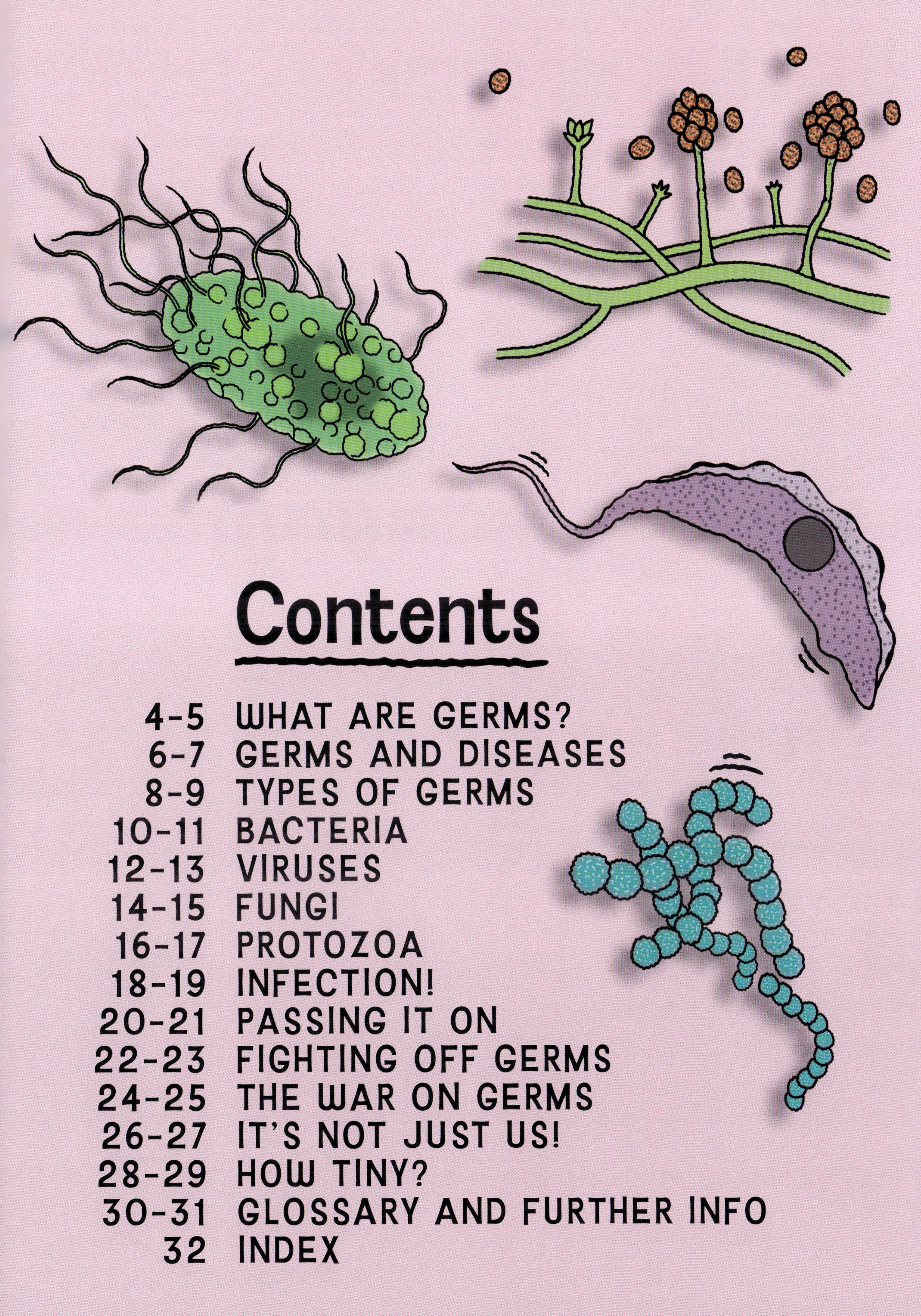

Contents

What are germs?

Germs are very small living things that can cause diseases.

Common cold germs

CHOOO!

When you catch a cold, for example, it's because tiny, invisible germs have found their way into your nose or mouth.

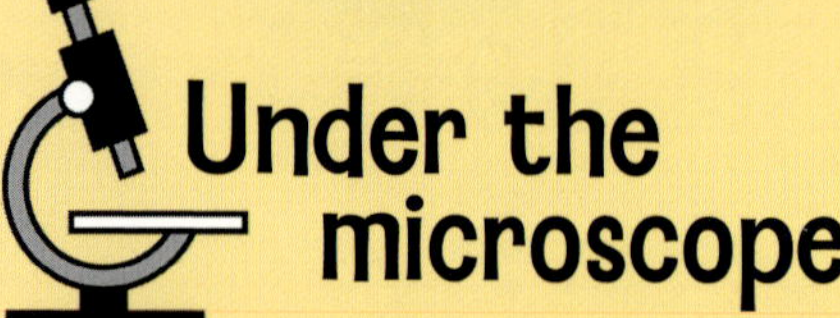

Why do they do that?!

When germs invade your body, they're not trying to be mean! They're just trying to survive.

This is what a common cold germ looks like close up.

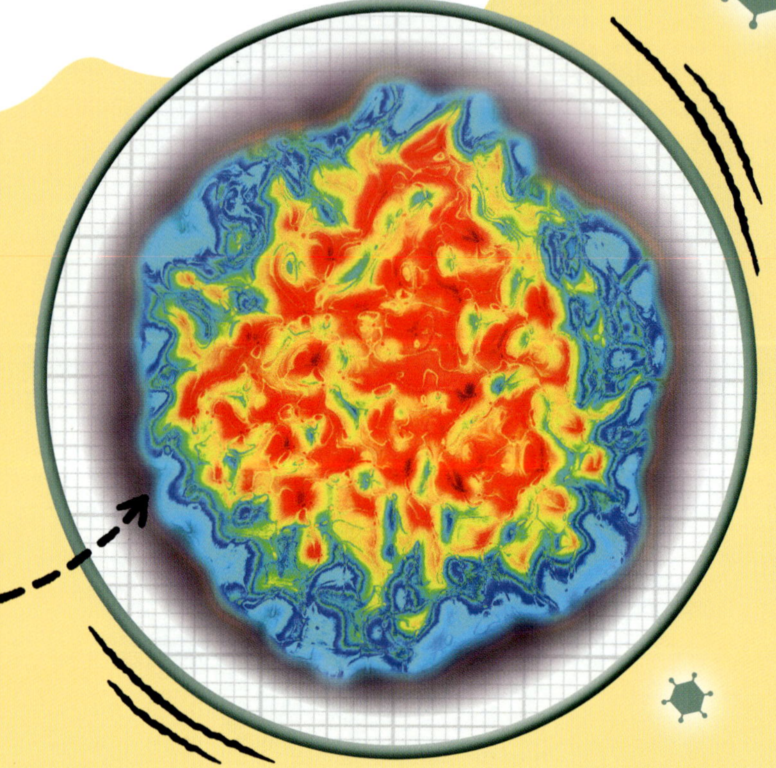

Staying alive

Like other living things, germs need food, water, and a place to live. They get these by invading – or infecting – another living thing. To a germ, you're just a nice, cozy home. But they can damage your body, making you sick.

Teeny weeny, you can't see me!

Since most germs are too small to see, they can sneak into your body without you noticing. They might be in the air you breathe, on your hands from touching a germy surface, or in your food. You only know about it when you start feeling unwell.

Marvels of the microscope

For thousands of years, no one knew what caused most diseases. It was a mystery! We discovered germs in the 1600s, when people invented the first microscopes.

Dutch microscope inventor Antonie van Leeuwenhoek was one of the first people to see microscopic germs in water and tooth plaque.

Germs and diseases

There are THOUSANDS of different types of germs, and they give us a huge range of different diseases.

Not too bad

Some are quite mild. Most people recover from them quickly.

- Colds
- Stomach bugs
- Warts
- Chicken pox

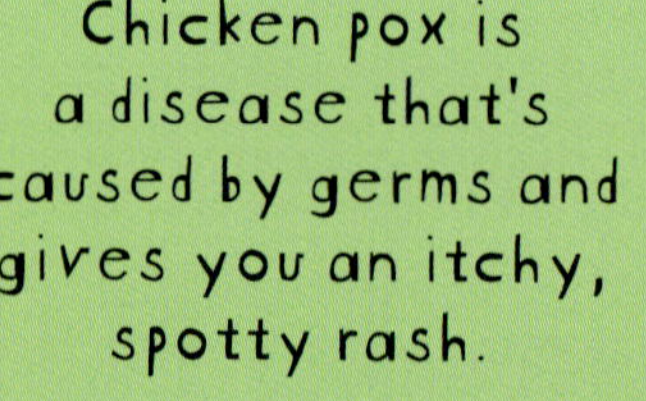
Chicken pox is a disease that's caused by germs and gives you an itchy, spotty rash.

Pretty unpleasant

Some are more serious.

- Flu can make some people very ill, especially if they're very old or very young.
- Mumps makes glands in your face swell up and can sometimes cause deafness or brain disease.

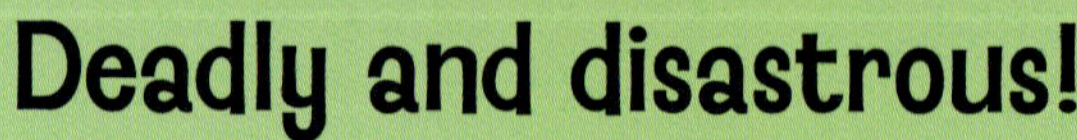

Deadly and disastrous!

And some diseases are seriously bad news, especially if they spread over a wide area.

- Malaria kills thousands of people every year.

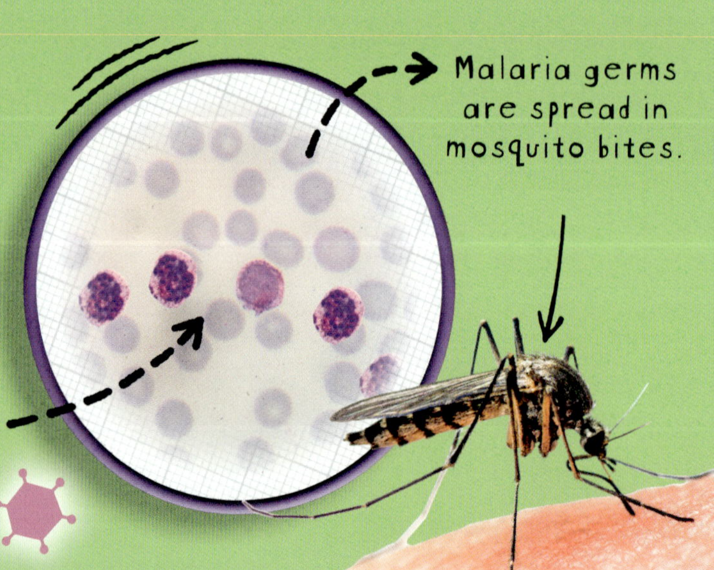
Malaria germs are spread in mosquito bites.

Plagues and pandemics

A dangerous disease called Covid-19 spread around the world, starting in 2019.

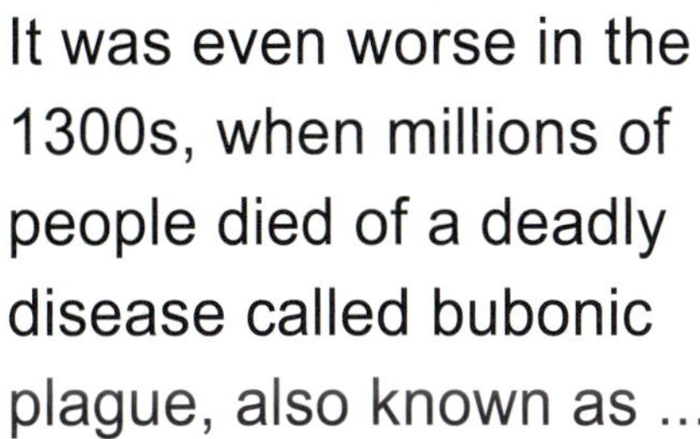

The coronavirus germ that causes Covid-19

It was even worse in the 1300s, when millions of people died of a deadly disease called bubonic plague, also known as ...

the Black Death.

Don't panic!

Long ago, before we knew how germs worked, it was hard to cure most diseases. Things are much better today! Germs are still a big problem, but we can treat a lot of them with modern medicines.

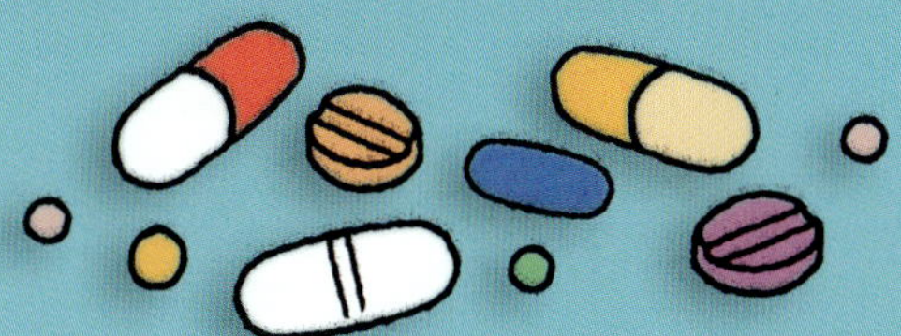

Medicines called antibiotics can cure some diseases, including bubonic plague. Phew!

Mouse medicine

In 16th-century Elizabethan England, people tried to cure warts by pressing half a dead mouse against them! (It didn't work.)

Types of germs

Germs can be divided into several types. Meet the main suspects!

Bacteria

Bacteria are very small, simple living things. They are single-celled, meaning they have only one cell each. (A human has over 30 trillion cells, so bacteria are pretty tiny!) They cause illnesses such as cholera, leprosy, and food poisoning.

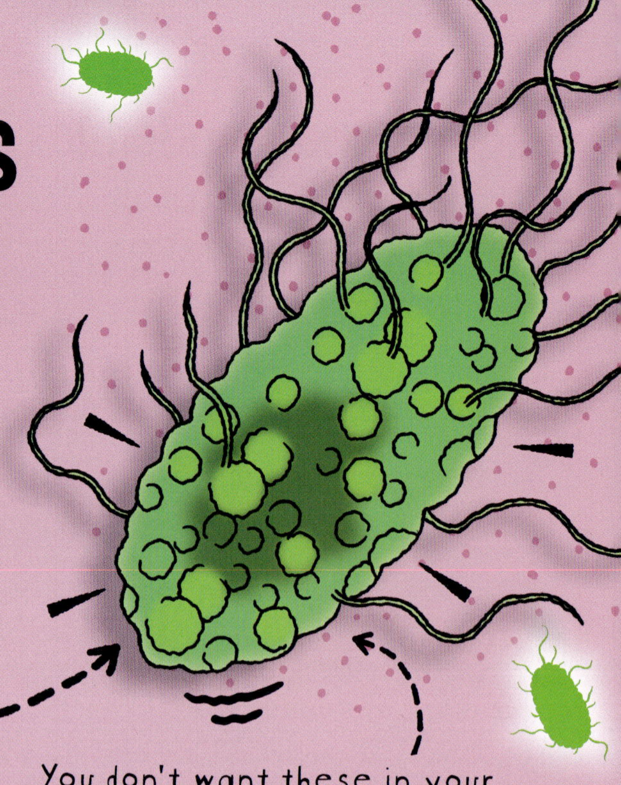

You don't want these in your lunch! They're Salmonella bacteria, which can cause food poisoning.

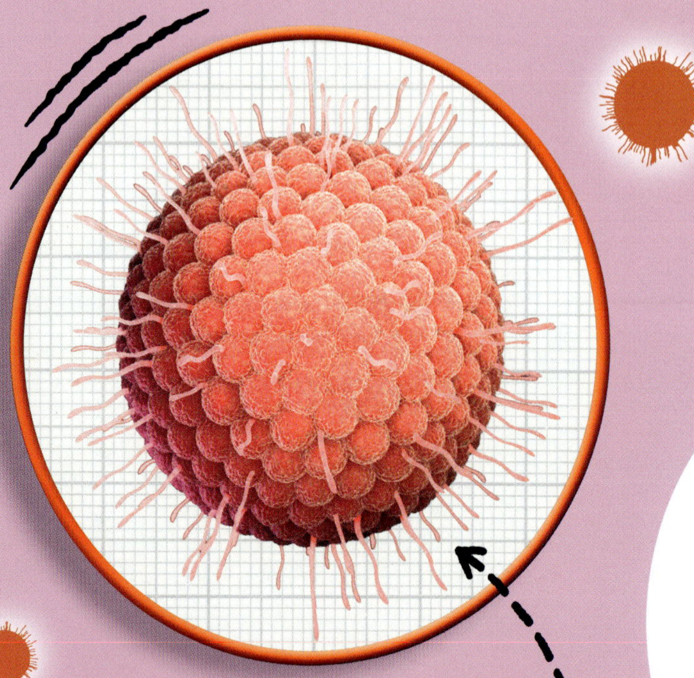

Fungi

Fungi are living things that include mushrooms and molds.

Some fungi, especially smaller and single-celled types, can cause diseases, for example, on the skin.

Viruses

Viruses are much smaller than bacteria and work by invading cells. They're responsible for the flu, colds, chicken pox, COVID-19, and many other diseases.

The virus behind chicken pox

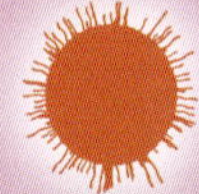

Protozoa

Protozoa are single-celled, like bacteria, but bigger and more complicated.

Don't forget us!

Besides the main four, there are also prions – weird, extremely small germs that cause a few rare diseases.

And there are parasitic worms that live inside people and animals, such as tapeworms and pinworms. They're gross and can make you ill, but they're too big to be counted as germs.

Bacteria

Let's take a closer look at bacteria. They are small, single-celled living things that can be found in soil, water, and sand; on rotting food; and inside plants and animals.

1 in 20

Not all bacteria are germs. In fact, of all the different species of bacteria, only about 1 in 20 causes disease. But some of those diseases are **HORRIBLE**. They include ...

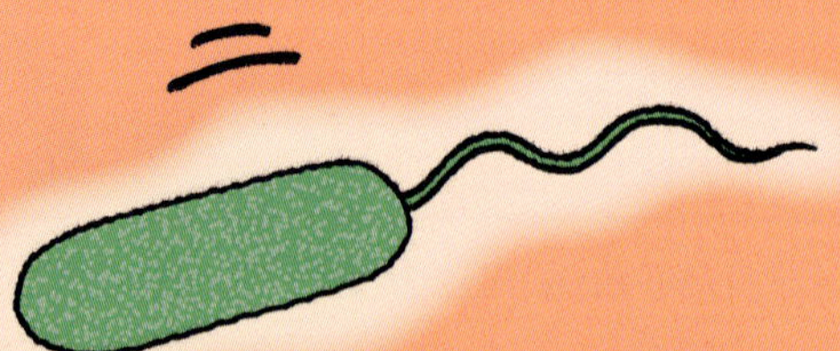
Cholera

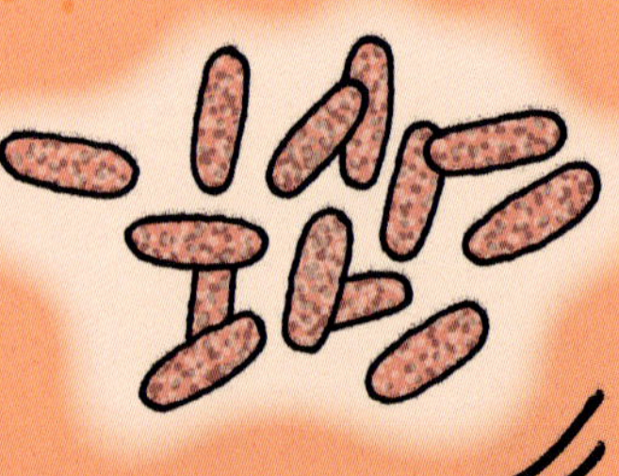
Bubonic plague

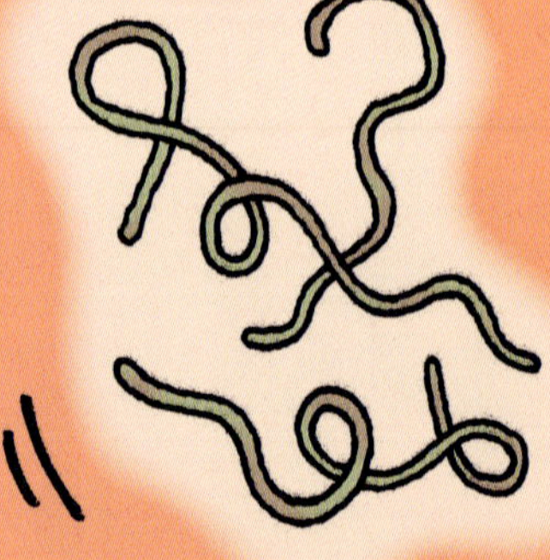
Lyme disease

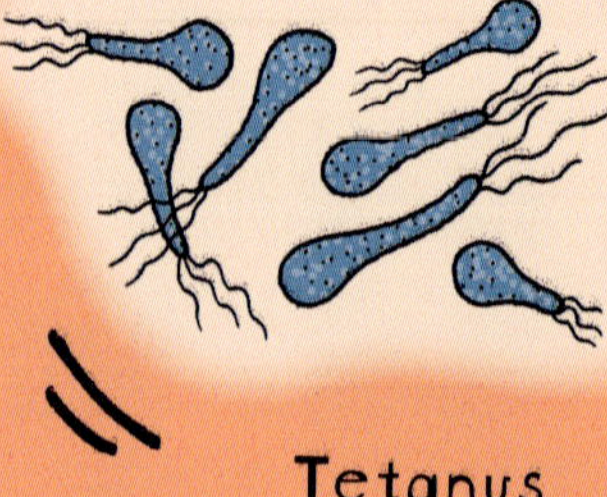
Tetanus

Leprosy

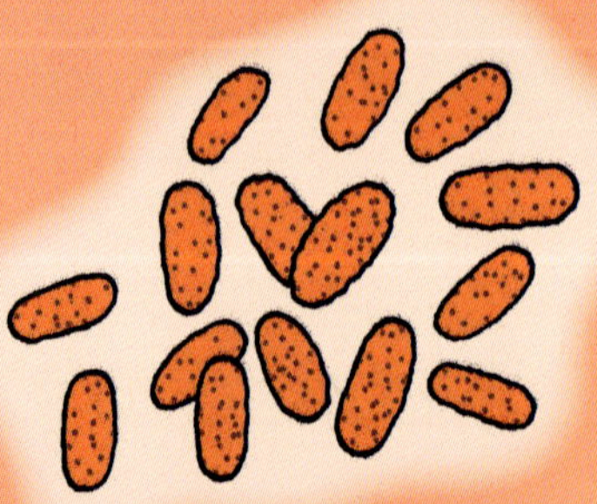
Whooping cough

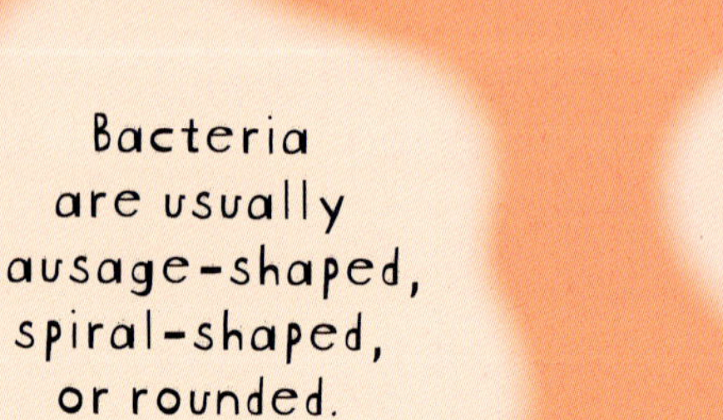

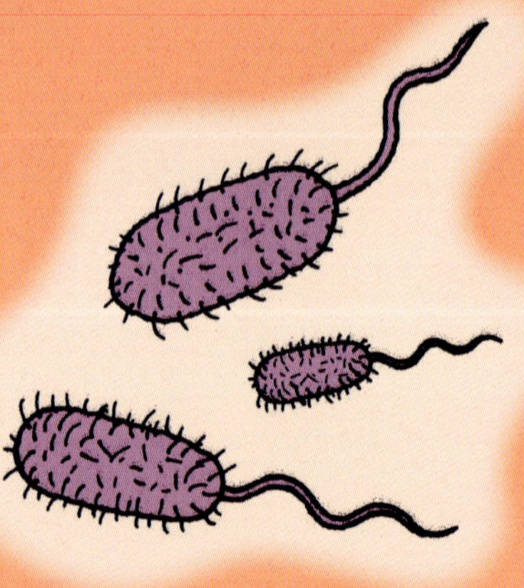
Typhus

Under the microscope

Cholera bacteria enter the body in food or water, and set up home in your intestines. As they breed and multiply, they release toxic chemicals that cause **TERRIBLE** diarrhea. It's so runny that you can easily lose too much water from your body, which can be deadly.

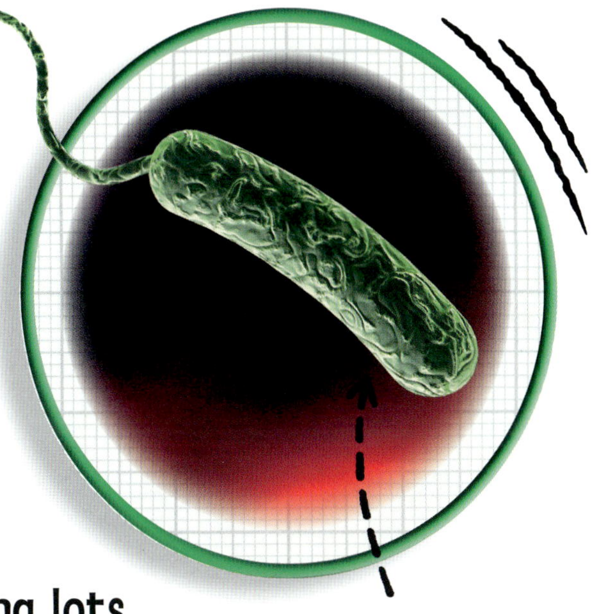

A single cholera bacterium

Luckily, you can survive by drinking lots of water and taking medicine.

Rotting teeth

Bacteria also live in your mouth and feed on what you eat. They cause tooth decay by releasing acid that eats away at your teeth.

Tooth bacteria

You know what to do!

Making copies

Like other living things, bacteria breed, or copy themselves. They do this by growing bigger, then splitting into two. If it has enough food, one bacterium can become millions in just a few hours.

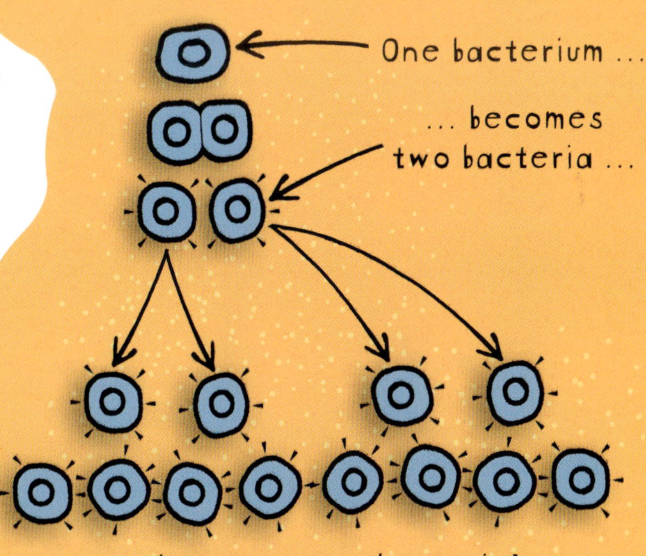

Viruses

Viruses are very, very small germs. Bacteria are pretty small. But viruses are TOTALLY TINY cell invaders.

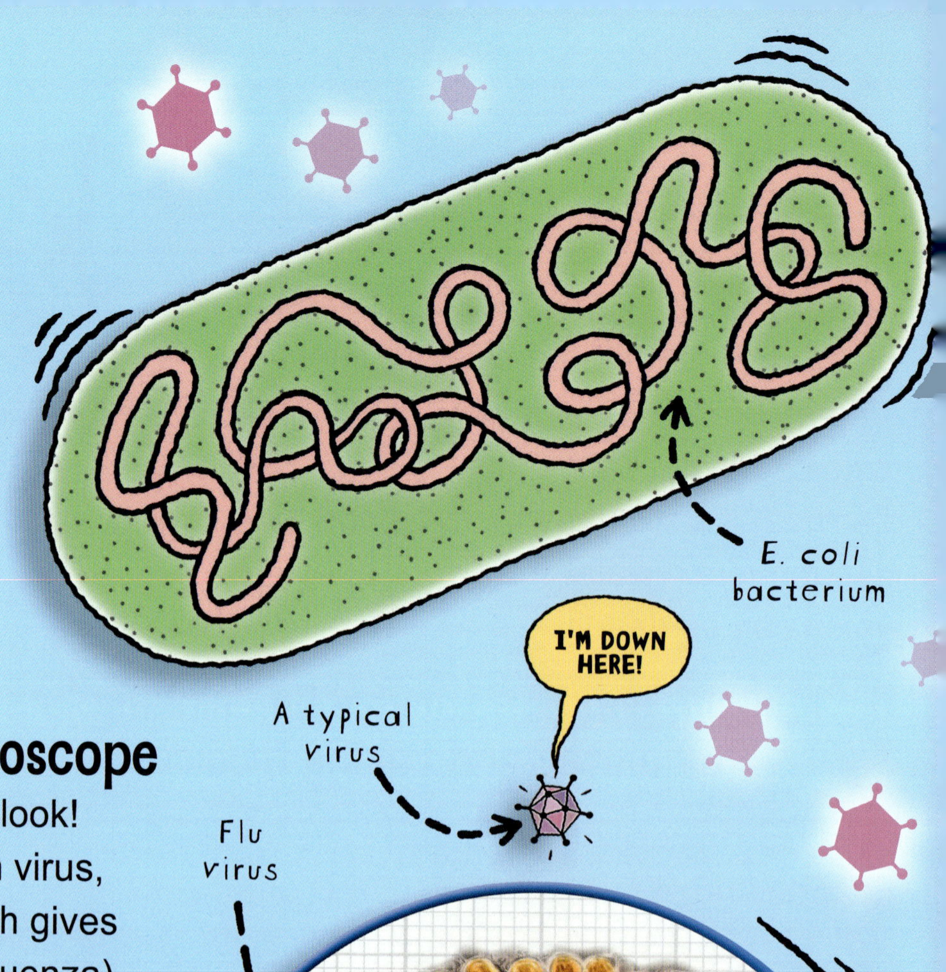

Under the microscope

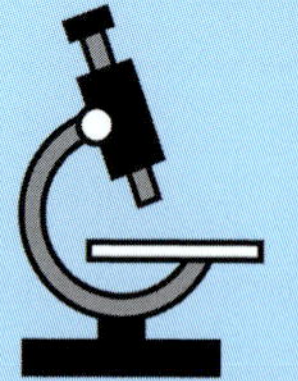

Time for a closer look! Here's a common virus, the flu virus, which gives you the flu (or influenza).

How viruses work

Here's what happens when you catch the flu, and flu viruses get inside your body.

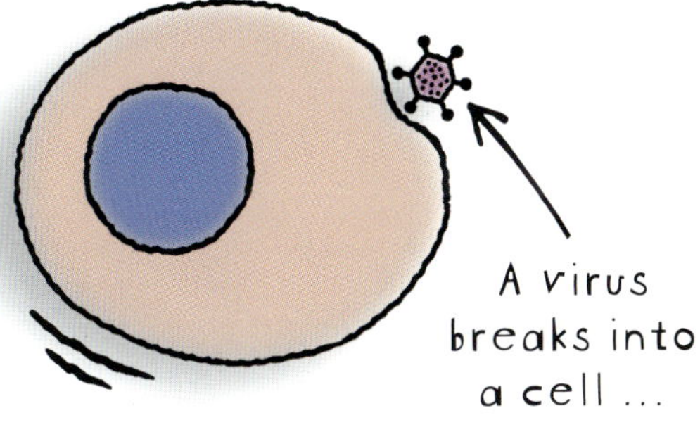

A virus breaks into a cell ...

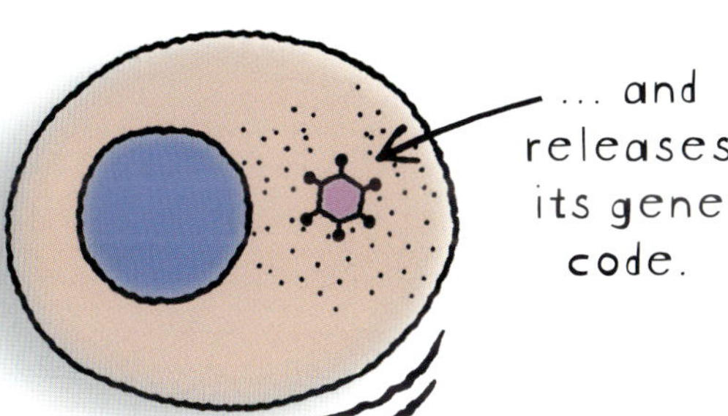

... and releases its gene code.

This makes the cell stop what it's doing and make lots more copies of the virus instead.

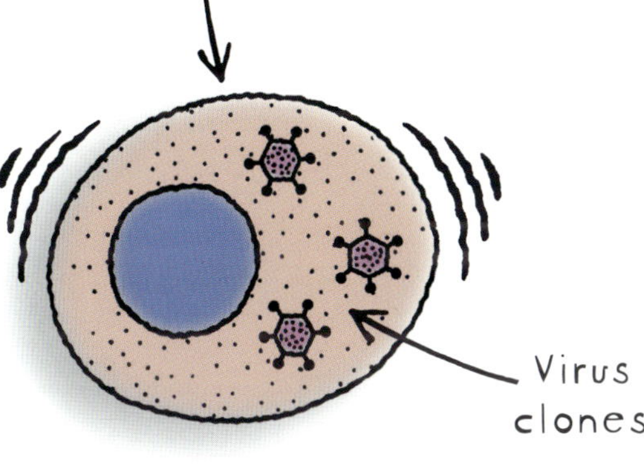

Virus clones

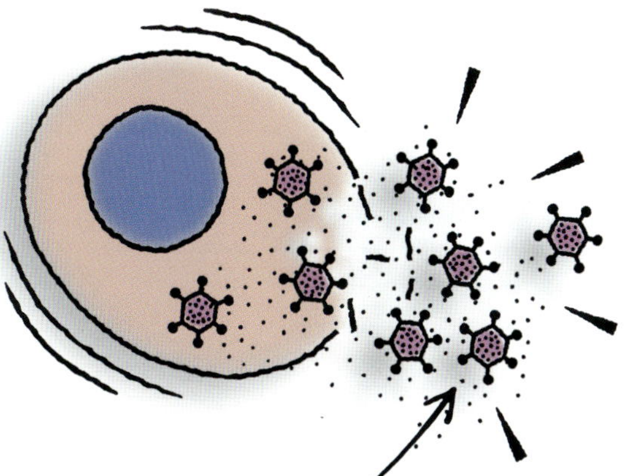

They burst out of the cell and set off to invade other cells.

I feel terrible!

Why does the flu make you feel so awful?

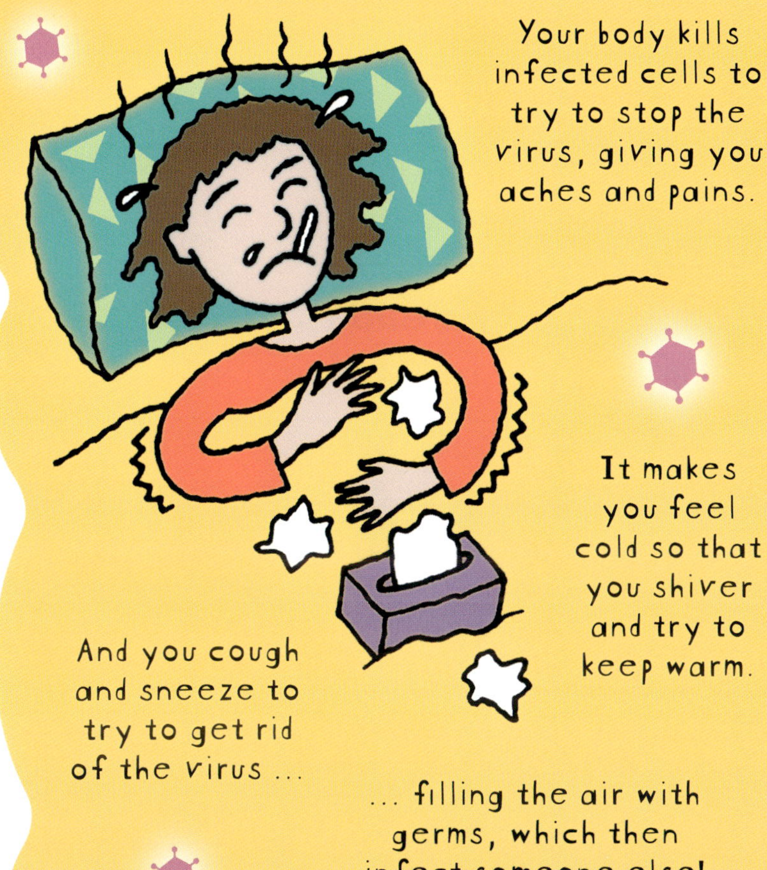

Your body kills infected cells to try to stop the virus, giving you aches and pains.

It makes you feel cold so that you shiver and try to keep warm.

And you cough and sneeze to try to get rid of the virus ...

... filling the air with germs, which then infect someone else!

All this makes you feel exhausted.

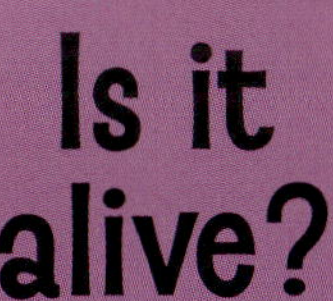

Is it alive?

Good question! It's hard to say if a virus is a living thing. When it's invading a cell, it's active – but when it's not, it doesn't do anything and is not "alive."

Fungi

You're probably familiar with fungi, especially if you like mushrooms! Yeast, used to make bread, is also a fungus. But there are some less friendly fungi out there too ...

The fungi family

Mushrooms and toadstools

Molds, which grow on rotting fruit, or damp bathroom walls

Yeasts

Fungi germs

Some yeasts and molds are germs that can grow in or on other living things. Ringworm, for example, lives on people's skin.

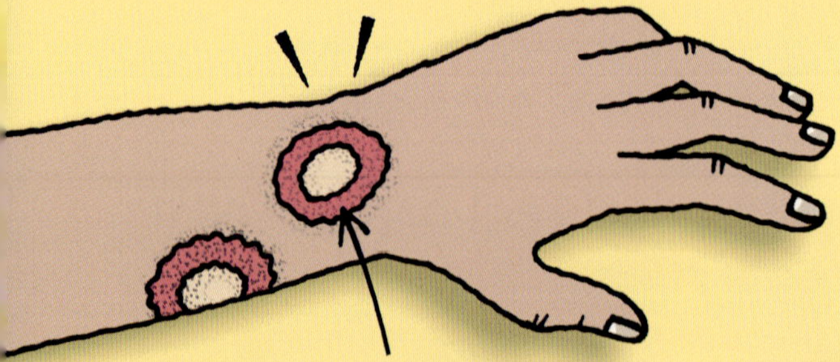

If you get ringworm, you won't see the microscopic fungi, just this ring-shaped rash.

Ringworm-causing fungi

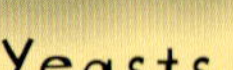

The fungi grow tiny threads called hyphae that reach down into the skin layers to feed.

Making more fungi

Some single-celled fungi breed by splitting in two, like bacteria. Others, like molds, release tiny spores. They float around in the air, then land somewhere and start growing. Breathing in spores can be bad for your lungs.

Protozoa

Last but not least, meet the protozoa! Like bacteria, they have only one cell each. But a protozoan is bigger and more complicated than a bacterium.

Killer germs

Many protozoa are harmless, but a few survive by invading humans or other host animals. This can cause nasty diseases, such as Chagas disease and sleeping sickness.

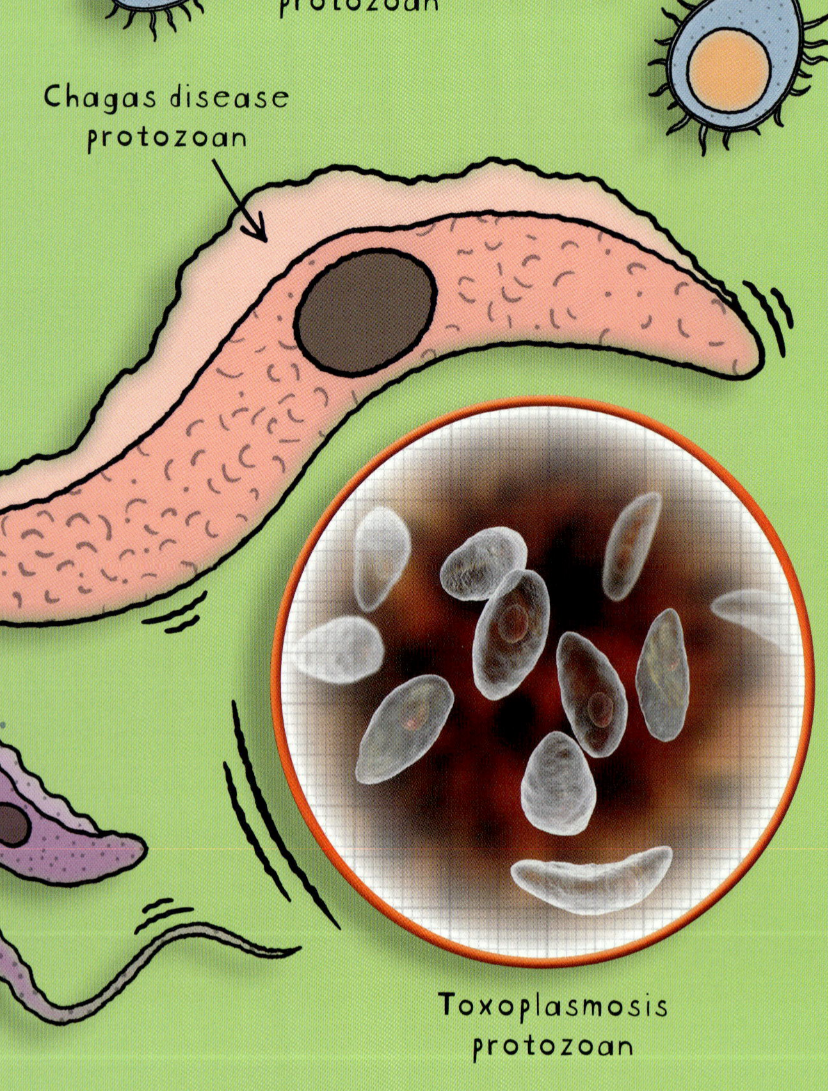

And one type is responsible for malaria, the **number 1 deadliest disease of all time**, which has killed more people than any other germ.

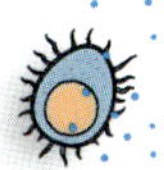

Host-hopping

Not content with one host, some protozoa have to hop in and out of two different animals to complete their life cycle. **Plasmodium**, which causes malaria, is one of these.

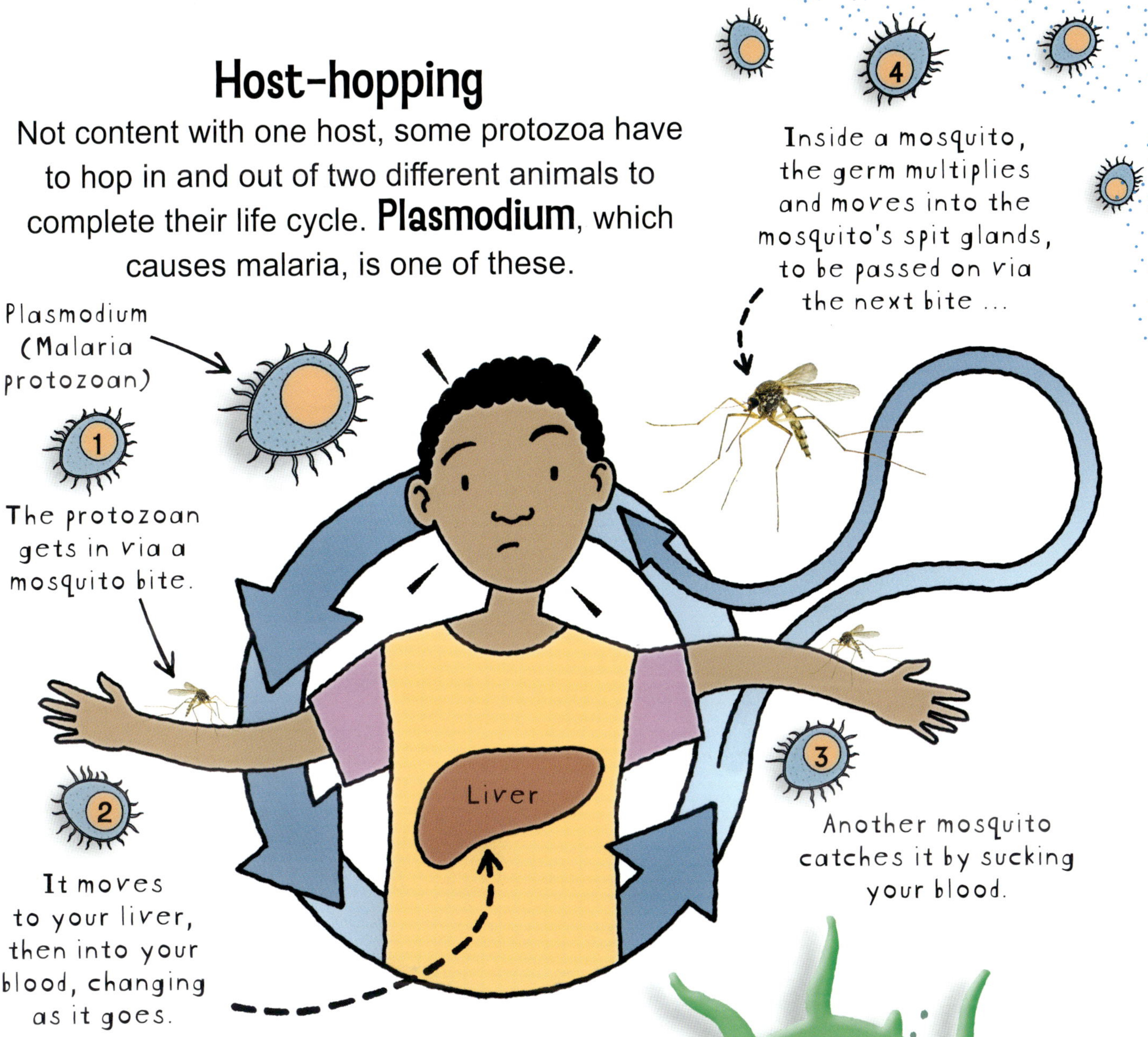

Plasmodium (Malaria protozoan)

1 The protozoan gets in via a mosquito bite.

2 It moves to your liver, then into your blood, changing as it goes.

Liver

3 Another mosquito catches it by sucking your blood.

4 Inside a mosquito, the germ multiplies and moves into the mosquito's spit glands, to be passed on via the next bite ...

Water dwellers

Many types of protozoa live in water and get into people's bodies when they drink it. They're a big problem in parts of the world where there isn't clean, running water on tap.

Dirty drinking water could contain protozoa.

Scary malaria

Some experts think malaria could have killed at least 20 billion people throughout history. It's an astonishing number, especially when you consider there have only been about 100 billion people ever!

Infection!

Don't panic, but ... there's a germ behind you! In fact, germs are all around us. We come into contact with them many times a day, both outdoors and indoors.

Germs move in

We don't get ill from every single germ we meet. The problems start when enough germs get in to start living and breeding. When this happens, it's called an infection.

BOO!

If these streptococcus bacteria get in your eye, you could have a sore, itchy eye infection.

I THINK I NEED THE DAY OFF ...

If you catch the flu or malaria, your whole body gets infected. You feel tired, achy, and weak all over.

Flu virus

Fungi often infect just one area, like this crumbly, yellow toenail infection.

Can you catch it?

A contagious disease is one you can catch from someone else, when germs from that person get into you. Some germs are much more contagious than others.

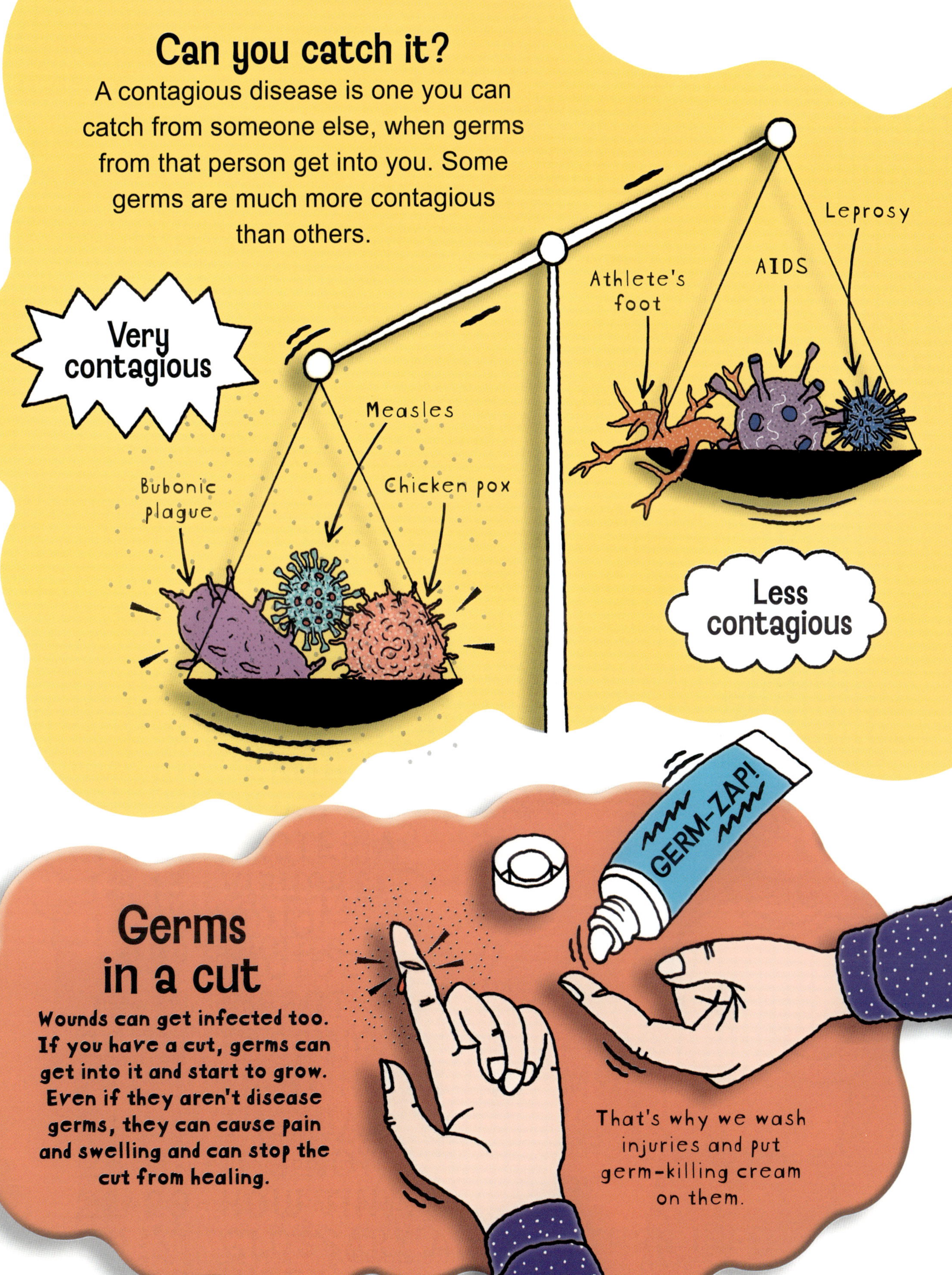

Germs in a cut

Wounds can get infected too. If you have a cut, germs can get into it and start to grow. Even if they aren't disease germs, they can cause pain and swelling and can stop the cut from healing.

That's why we wash injuries and put germ-killing cream on them.

Passing it on

To keep on living and breeding, germs need to get from one person to another.

And they have some GENIUS ways to do that!

Coughs and sneezes . . .

Have you ever wondered why colds and the flu make you sneeze and cough? If you think about it, it's a great way to make sure other people get sprayed with your germs!

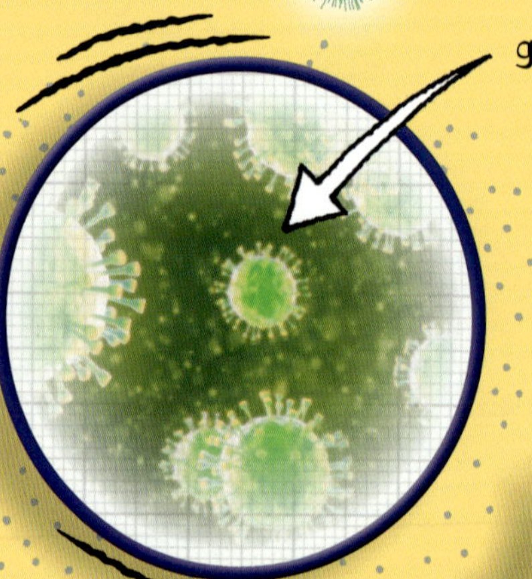

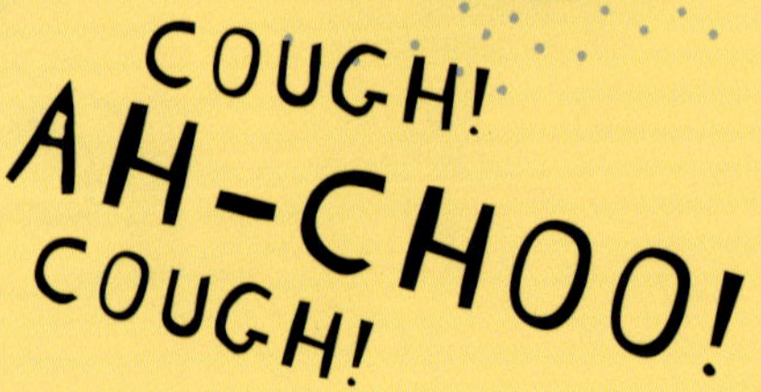

RESULT:

Snotty, germ-filled droplets get fired far away from you. Other people breathe them in, and the germs spread!

Cholera poop

Some germs have even ickier ways of spreading. Remember cholera from pages 10–11? It gives you bad diarrhea because explosive poop is harder to clean and contain. That means it can more easily get into the water system. Someone else swims in it or drinks it, and the germs get passed on.

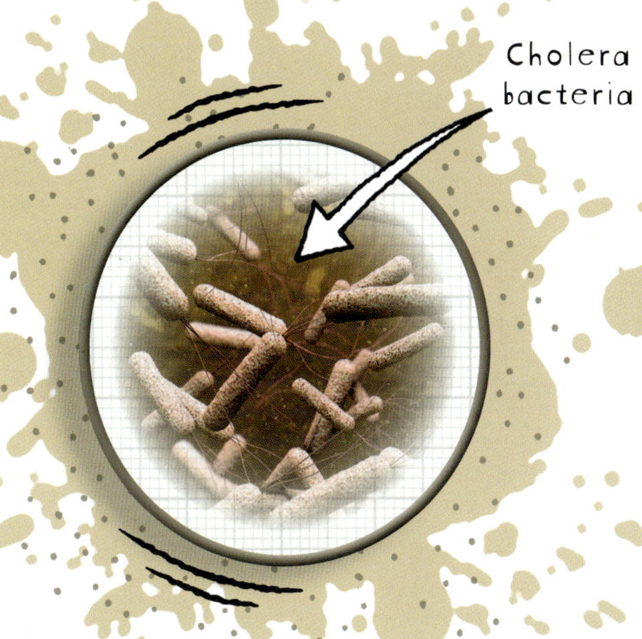

Stop the spread!

The germ that caused the Covid-19 pandemic used coughing and breathing as methods of spreading. That's why wearing face masks and keeping a 6-foot (2-meter) distance between people helped to stop it from being passed on.

New germs

As germs copy themselves again and again, they can gradually change and evolve. This creates new forms, called strains, that can cause new diseases. Covid-19, for example, is caused by a new type of coronavirus that appeared in 2019. As the pandemic went on, new strains of COVID-19 itself emerged as well.

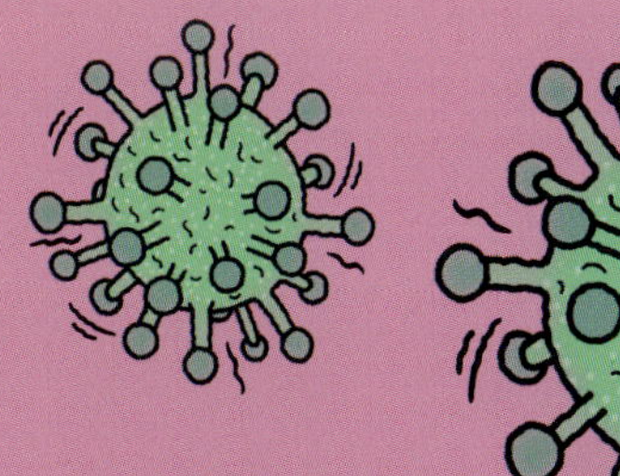
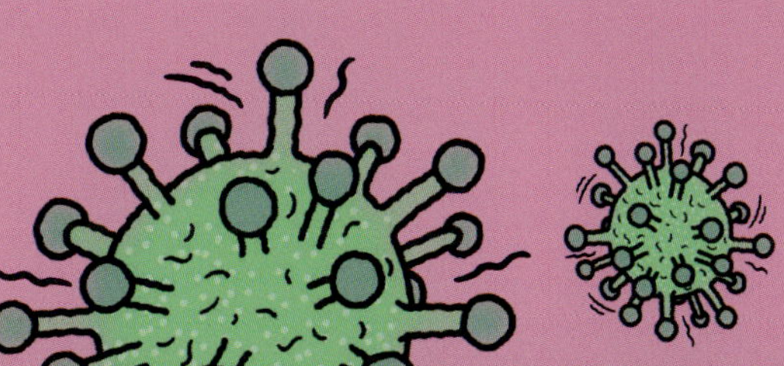
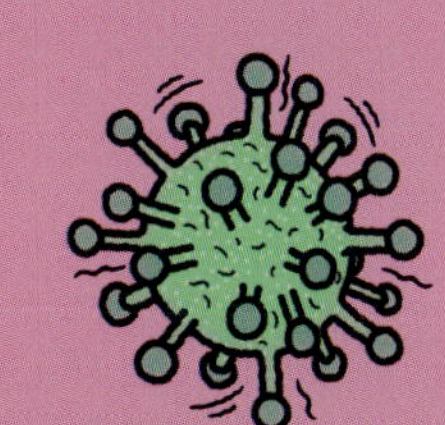
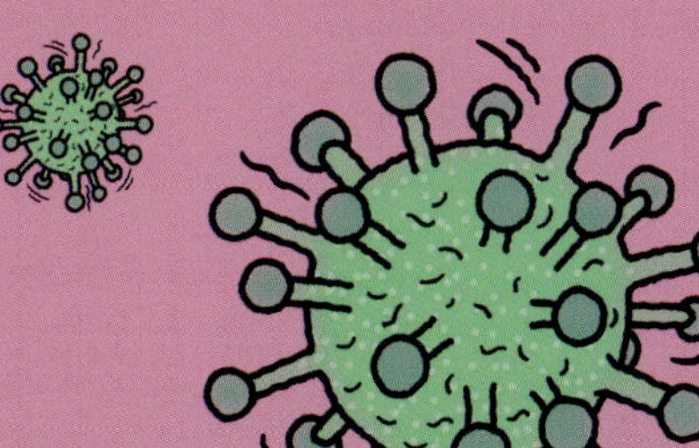

Fighting off germs

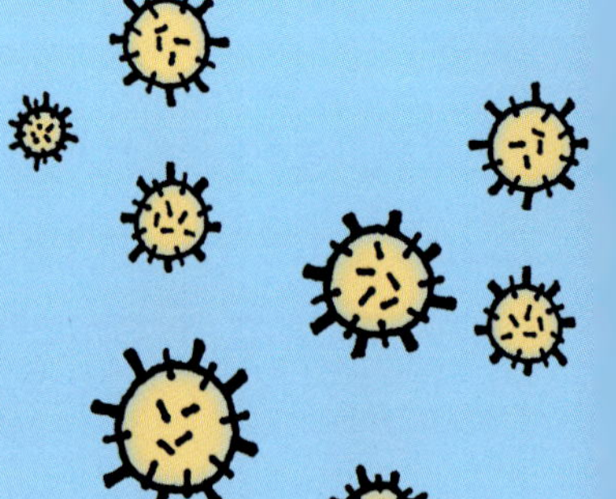

Germs are smart – but so are we! Over millions of years, we've evolved a way to protect ourselves from them. It's called …

The immune system!

The body's immune system works to keep germs out and kill the ones that do get in. It has many different parts that all do their share.

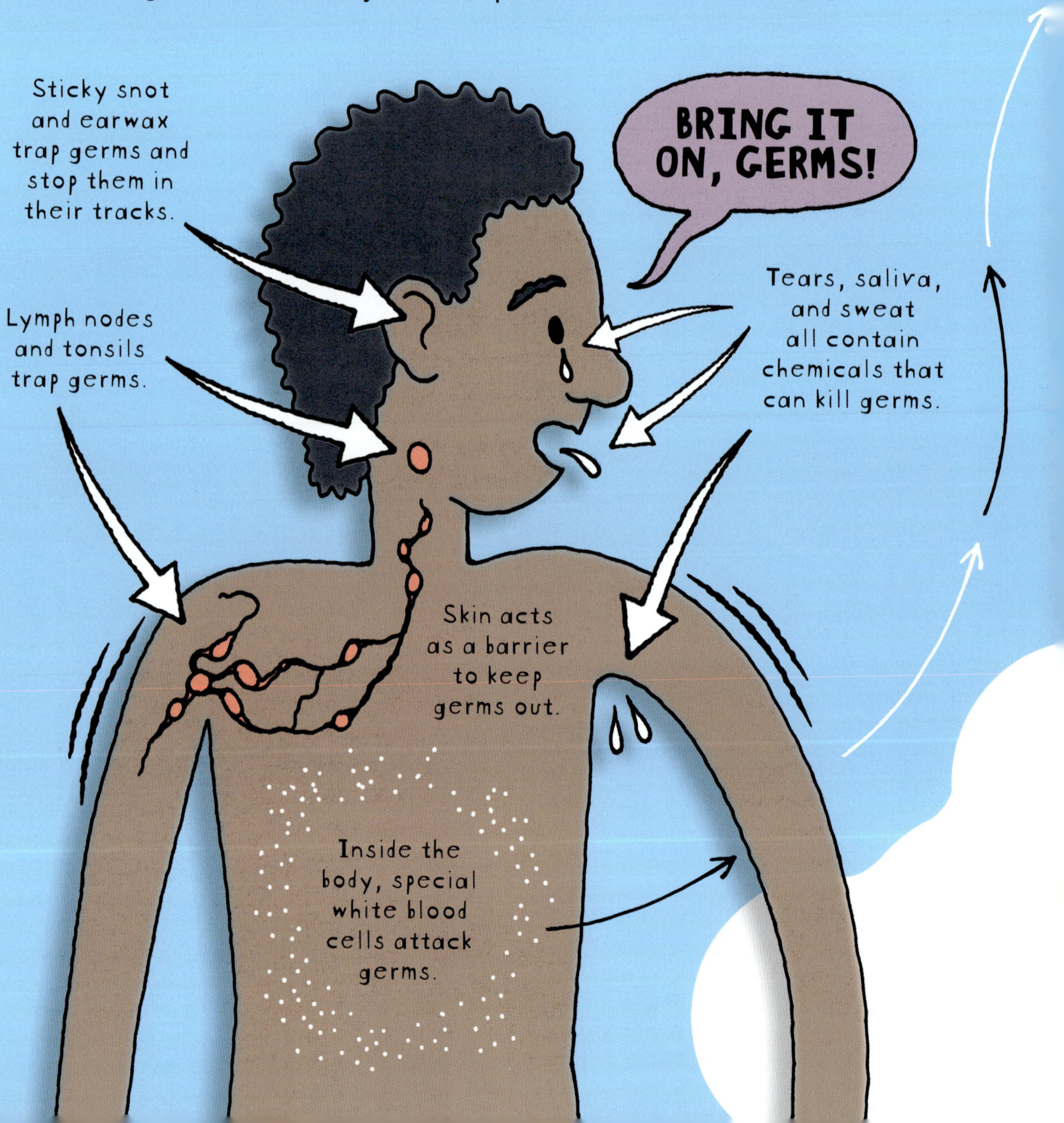

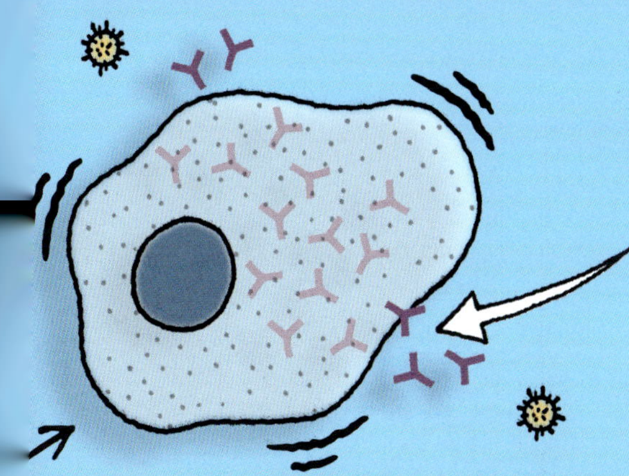

Some white blood cells make antibodies that disable germs ...

... and others swallow germs up.

I've seen you before!

White blood cells don't just kill germs, they also remember them. If you get chicken pox, the white blood cells fight the virus and learn to recognize it. Then, if chicken pox germs get in again, the clever white blood cells can spot them and fight them off before they can spread.

HELLO AGAIN!

Chicken pox virus

In the United States, kids have to get a chicken pox vaccine before school. Almost no one gets it anymore!

Vaccination

Vaccination protects you from a disease you haven't had.

1 A vaccine contains a disabled germ, or part of a germ, that can't cause disease.

2 The vaccine is injected into the body or sometimes taken as a pill.

3 The immune system learns to recognize the germs. Then, if the active germs come along, it can fight them off.

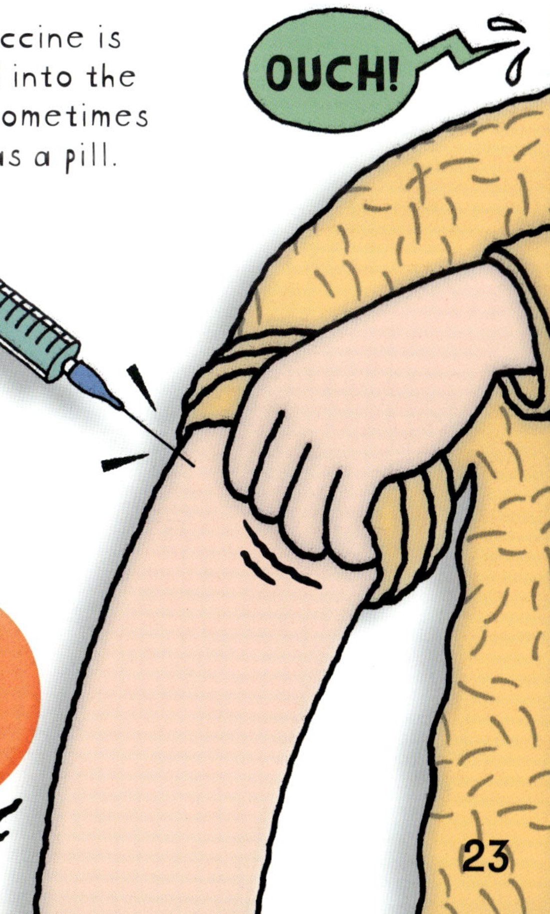

Keep it working

Getting enough sleep and eating healthily keep your immune system working as well as it can.

The war on germs

Of course, it's not just your body that can kill germs.

Keep it clean!

Cleaning gets rid of most germs. For example, soap washes germs off your hands. They are carried away down the drain and get destroyed by modern sewage treatment systems. Hand sanitizer and disinfectant can kill germs on the spot.

Hospitals have to be VERY clean to make sure they're safe – especially operating rooms and surgical tools.

Safe to eat

You can also kill most germs with heat. Some raw food, like chicken, can contain germs, but cooking it all the way through kills them.

And keeping fresh food in the fridge or freezer stops germs from growing.

Protection

We also have medicines that kill germs.

This athlete's foot cream kills fungi.

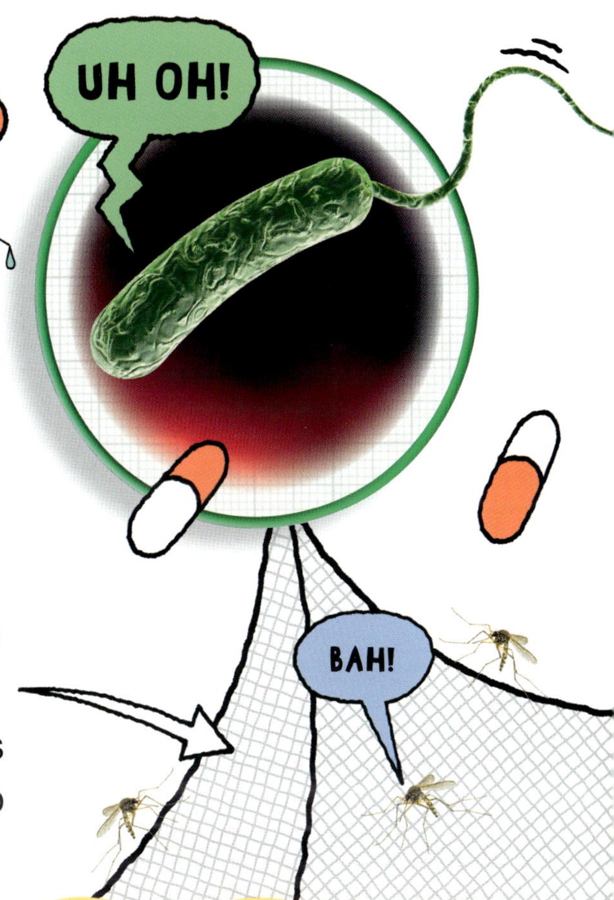

Antibiotics kill bacteria, so they can be used to treat diseases like cholera.

And if germs are spread by mosquitoes, mosquito nets can help keep them away.

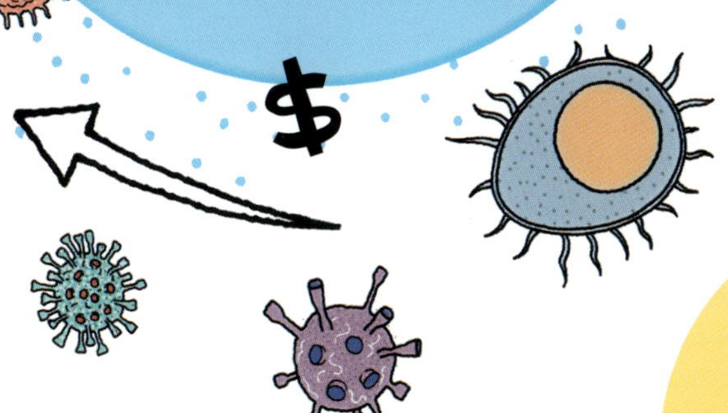

Around the world

All these things cost money. That means poorer countries often have worse problems with germs and diseases than rich countries do.

Banished forever

Do you know anyone who's had smallpox? Probably not – because it's gone! Using vaccinations and germ-control methods, the virus that causes this nasty disease has been wiped out. It now exists only in a few science labs.

Smallpox virus

Smallpox caused a fever, large spots (or "pox"), and sometimes blindness or death.

It's not just us!

Other animals can get diseases from germs, too, and so can plants. Even germs can catch germs!

Animals

Animals can get some of the same diseases as we do. For example, cats, dogs, pigs, and birds can all get the flu – although they usually catch slightly different forms of the virus.

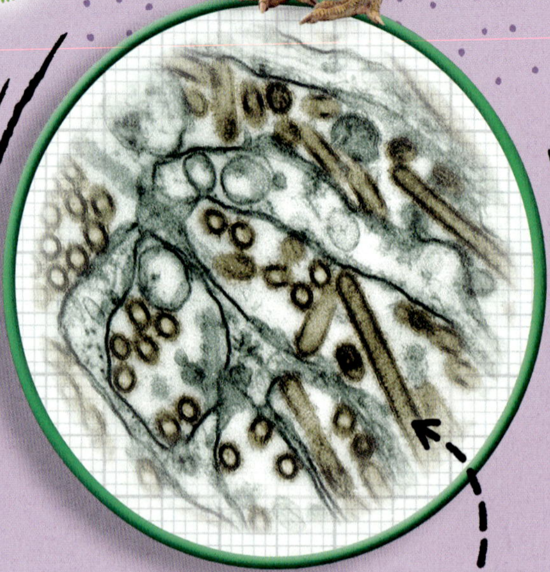

SNIFFLE! SNIFFLE!

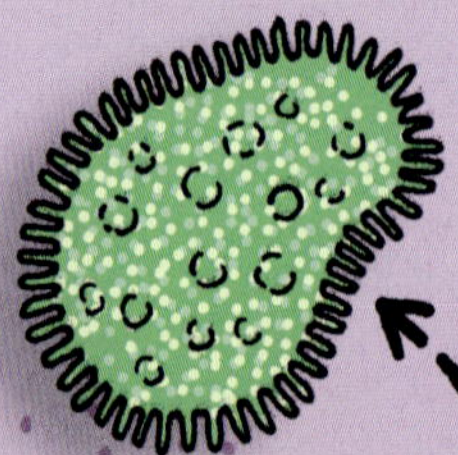

Dog flu virus

Bird flu virus

SNIFFLE! SNIFFLE!

WHAT ARE THEY TRYING TO DO TO ME?

Animals can get vaccinations too. If you have a cat or dog, it might get vaccinations every year for the flu and other illnesses.

Plants

Plants and trees can catch viruses, bacteria, and fungi. They're often spread by insects flying from one plant to the next.

If you're an oak tree, you don't want to catch the bacteria that cause "drippy nut"!

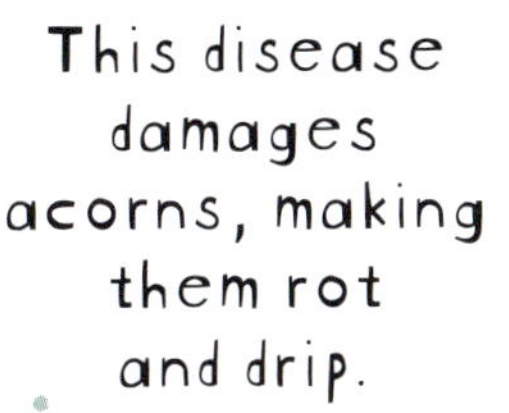

Healthy acorns

Acorns affected by drippy nut disease

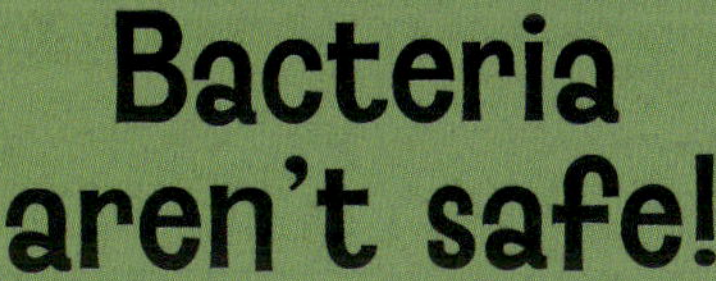

Bacteria aren't safe!

There are even viruses that attack and invade bacteria. And some molds make chemicals that kill bacteria.

Mind control

Toxoplasmosis, or toxo, is caused by a protozoan germ. It's common in cats, and mice sometimes catch it from cat poop.

What's really weird is that the germ changes how mice behave – a bit like the zombie ant fungus on page 15. It makes mice less scared of cats so it's easier for cats to catch them! So for cats, toxo can be a good thing. For mice, not so much!

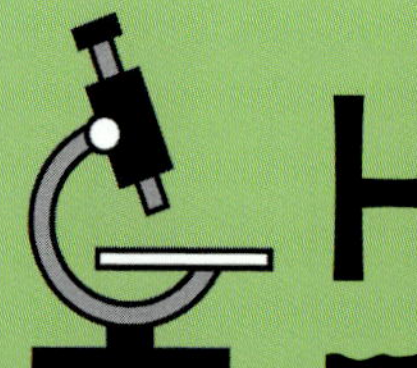

How tiny?

All the germs in this book are very, very small – so small you can't see them. But just HOW small are they? Here you can actually see some of them compared to one another and to a human hair.

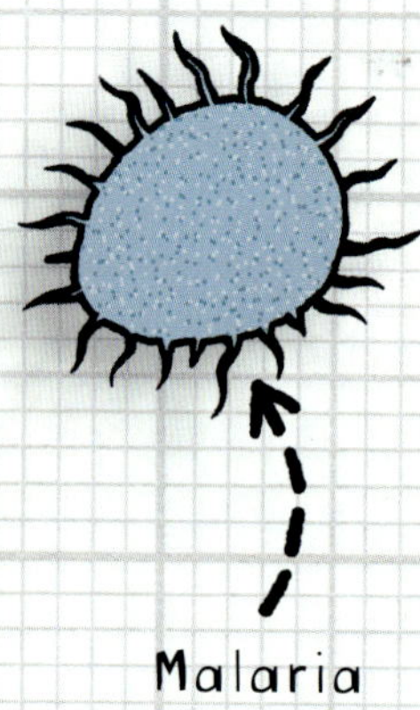

Micro measures

For measuring normal everyday things, we use centimeters, inches, meters, or feet. But for really tiny things like cells, scientists use a different unit: the micron (or micrometer).

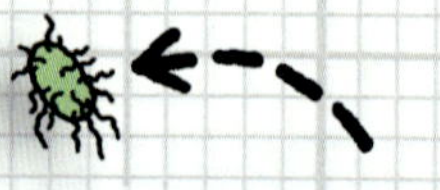

One micron is **1,000th** of a millimeter.

So there are **1,000** microns in a millimeter … and **1** million microns in a meter.

The micron symbol is:

White blood cell

Tooth bacterium

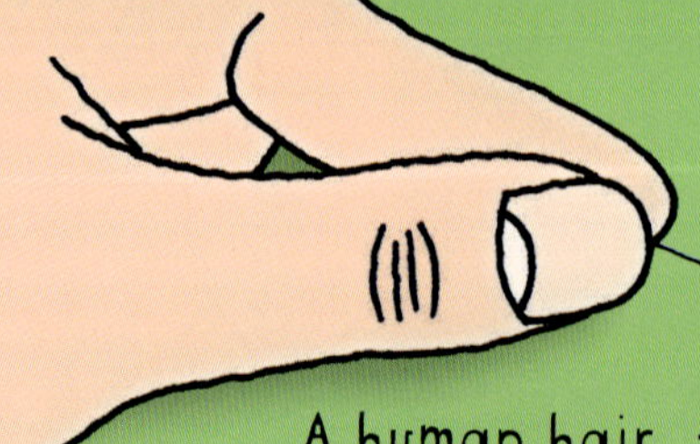

A human hair, for example, is around 80 µm thick.

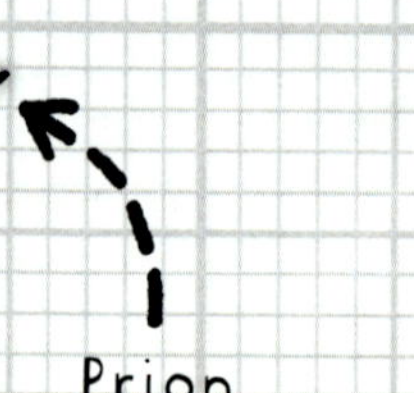

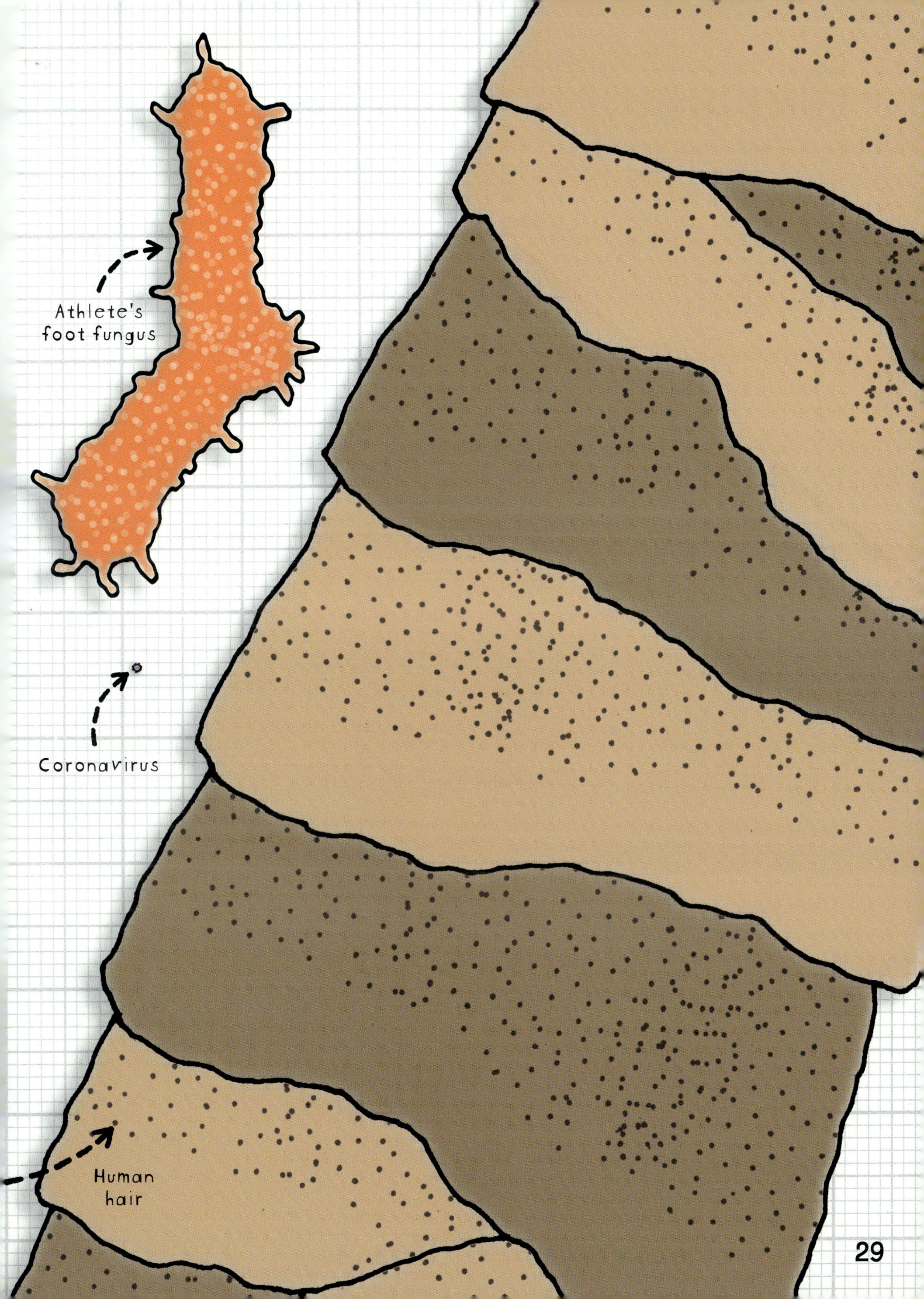
Athlete's
foot fungus
Coronavirus
Human
hair

Glossary

AIDS A type of illness, caused by a virus, that harms the immune system.

antibiotics Medicines that kill bacteria and are used to treat many diseases.

antibodies Substances that white blood cells release to attack germs.

athlete's foot A foot infection caused by a fungus that gives you sore, flaky skin.

breed To reproduce or have babies.

cells The tiny building blocks that make up living things.

Chagas disease A disease caused by a protozoan and spread by insects.

clone A living thing that is an exact copy of another living thing.

contagious A contagious disease can spread from one person to another.

diarrhea Very watery, runny poop that can be caused by some illnesses and germs.

E. coli A type of bacterium that is sometimes harmless but can cause illness.

evolve How species of living things gradually change over time.

gene code Information inside viruses or cells that controls what they do.

host A person or animal that is infected by a protozoan or parasite.

hyphae The branching, root-like parts of a fungus.

immune system The body system that works to keep out or kill germs.

infect Germs infect you when they get into your body and start breeding and growing.

influenza The scientific name for the flu. ("Flu" is short for influenza.)

lymph nodes Small, bean-shaped body parts containing white blood cells that kill germs.

micrometer Another name for a micron.

micron A tiny unit of measurement, one-thousandth of a millimeter long.

pandemic A disease outbreak that spreads across many countries or the whole world.

parasite A living thing that lives on or inside another living thing and takes food from it.

plaque A thin layer of food and bacteria that forms on teeth after eating.

saliva Another name for spit, the liquid in the mouth.

sleeping sickness A dangerous disease caused by a type of protozoan and spread by tsetse flies.

smallpox A disease that causes large spots, or "pox," and was once common but has now been wiped out.

species A particular type of living thing.

spores Tiny, seed-like parts released by fungi, which can grow into new fungi.

strain A new form or variety of a virus or other germ.

tonsils Two small body parts in the throat that catch and kill germs.

white blood cell A type of blood cell that attacks and destroys germs in the body.

Further information

Websites

https://discoverycentre.telethonkids.org.au/science-activities-for-kids/germs/

Discovery Centre germs page with activities and games.

https://www.sciencephoto.com/dennis-kunkel-microscopy-collection

A collection of cool microscope pictures of germs and cells.

https://www.mrsec.psu.edu/sites/mrsec.psu.edu/files/pathogen_modeling.pdf

Make realistic models of a range of germs.

Books

Vaccinated

By Sarah Ridley (Franklin Watts, 2021)

The Germ Lab: The Gruesome Story of Deadly Diseases

By Richard Platt (Kingfisher, 2020)

Alice Dent and the Incredible Germs

By Gwen Lowe (Chicken House, 2018)

Plague

By Ben Hubbard (Franklin Watts, 2020)

Every effort has been made by the Publishers to ensure that the websites in this book are suitable for children, that they are of the highest educational value, and that they contain no inappropriate or offensive material. However, because of the nature of the Internet, it is impossible to guarantee that the contents of these sites will not be altered. We strongly advise that Internet access is supervised by a responsible adult.

Index